Anatomy of Autism

A Pocket Guide for Educators, Parents, and Students

Diego M. Peña

DEDICATION

This book is dedicated to Amanda Johnson, my communication partner and behavioral therapist extraordinaire! This book would not be possible without you.

CONTENTS

ACKNOWLEDGMENTS

I have many reasons to be thankful. First, I would like to say I'm thankful for my family, my mom and dad. They are always supportive of my accomplishments. When I achieve my goals they make me feel so special and proud. I have a great mom who fought for my communication. Without her, I would not have a voice. A huge thank you to Soma Mukhopadhyay for starting me on my journey to communication. I am grateful to Ido for writing the foreword. Thanks, friend! Next, I am thankful for Team Diego. This is all the therapists (Amanda Johnson, Katie Anawalt, Kimberly Perry, Ali Steers, Brynne Blumstein) and teachers (Mrs. Wood, Mrs. Medina, Mrs. Narasaki, Mrs. Kitchen) who dedicate themselves to me to help me have a better life. They work so hard to teach me new skills to be successful in life. I am lucky to have them. I really appreciate the administrators at my school—Carol Bjordahl, Jo Kolb, and John Reilley—who have provided the appropriate supports for me to thrive academically. Finally, I am thankful for my communication. I was born without a voice but was given one through alternative ways. Technology saved me from a life of silence.

FOREWORD
By Ido Kedar

Diego Peña is a lucky nine-year-old boy with autism. He could have been stuck not communicating his entire life, like too many people who cannot speak and have limited control over their motor system. People often remain trapped because they look like they don't understand, they act oddly and they are assumed by the experts to not be processing speech. But Diego, despite his autism, is a fully included general education student who thrives in a regular school and is obviously intelligent, as his writing here proves.

When I was Diego's age I knew no other people with autism who typed to communicate. Now I know many. Diego has been able to benefit from the experiences of autistic people who went on a similar journey before him. Now he finds his own way and overcomes his own obstacles. Yet, Diego is changing not only his own life, but also the lives of autistic people who will follow in his footsteps. In school he is an ambassador, educating his classmates and faculty through his own example about the potential of people with autism.

The insights found in these pages reflect my experiences and those of other people with autism clearly and succinctly. I am proud of Diego for undertaking this task to help improve the lives of those with autism and their loving families.

1 INTRODUCTION

The reality of autism is generally not understood by the neurotypical world. The many things that make us autistic should not be seen as something flawed. We are capable of being heroes, but our abilities are as unique as our disabilities. So more people need to look at what we can do and not at what we can't do. Being on a spectrum means that autism affects us differently, making us unique. In this book, I talk about the sensory system, communication, and motor system. The sensory system for an autistic person creates many realities of hardships in daily life. Communication is difficult but is possible with the right tools. Motor planning is challenging because the brain and body are disconnected. This book is intended to change the assumptions people have of autism!

2 THE MYSTERIOUS AUTISM SPECTRUM

The autism spectrum is used to identify how severe the symptoms of autism are for an individual that has been diagnosed. This same system is also used to determine deficits. The term spectrum doesn't have to be negative. It can be used as an indicator of how to provide support to make us successful as we are without the need to change who we are meant to be. The spectrum allows us to be unique and we should be treated as individuals. I have experienced both judgement and freedom. When I was judged my wings were bound by the low expectations and I could not succeed. Now that I am free to be autistic, I soar. Having the spectrum is important for understanding but should be only used for understanding. The diagnosis of autism is a challenge to cope with already, so I advise against using labels to limit us beyond our born limitations. No person should be only known by a bunch of technical words written in a book. These words begin us on our autistic journey and they are not words to live by. Professionals and labels are important because we need access to services, but that shouldn't cost us our dignity. Anyone reading these words, I only ask that you look deeper into who we are as a person and not just on the surface.

3 HOUSTON, WE HAVE A SENSORY PROBLEM

Imagine being trapped in a room with everything you hate. Now picture how that makes your feel? Does your body feel calm and relaxed or bursting with anxiety? My guess is you chose bursting with anxiety. Welcome to the autistic sensory experience. Our sensory system is in constant overdrive which makes it a challenge to participate in our everyday environments. We possess the same senses but the autistic brain experiences everything intensely, making it almost impossible to cope. Really the truth is my autistic behaviors are my coping behaviors because the anxiety pushes my body to react constantly to the sensory system. My sensory system has the most difficulty with noise. I hear everything intensely at all times because I can't filter out what's going on in the background. This is the most difficult to cope with. I also struggle with seeing, touch, and taste. I don't have any challenges with smell, but some autistics do. I see things intensely and this can be very distracting because I'm a visual stimmer. Touch can be good or bad depending on how regulated I am but generally I like physical contact. Taste is tricky because I like the taste of many things but I can't handle the texture. Every autistic has different sensory experiences with some similarities that show our struggle. So in the future when you encounter an autistic person, I promise we aren't trying to be obnoxious.

4 JUST DON'T LEAVE ME SPEECHLESS

It is my right as a person to always have communication no matter how controversial it is. Communication is vital to life, but is taken for granted by those that are with a voice. Communication is more than talking; it's the lifeline to love, friendship, needs, and success. Do injustices happen to the autistic community? The answer is yes, and it's because our communication challenges are misunderstood. My personal experience is that I was born without the capability to talk due to apraxia. This also makes it hard for me to start a jovial chat or respond to your hellos. Trust me, I want to talk to you. My inability to speak is confused for my intelligence. I do have a voice, I speak with a Talker (my iPad), and I get to share my ability as a thinker like everyone else. I love writing because I get to be creative, witty, and free of autism. Writing is a release from being trapped inside this body. For those of us without a voice, augmentative and alternative communication (AAC) is a great way to provide communication. The autistics with a voice also need help with communication and sharing their thinking person too. Working on communication in a meaningful way should be a priority when working with us. There is nothing worse than being left out of the conversation. Talk to us please; we love to be included. You have the power to make a difference in how people judge a person with autism.

5 GET YOUR MOTOR RUNNIN'

It is a challenge for some autistics to get their body to work with them. This is called motor planning and it is also the demon of apraxia. My brain and body don't communicate messages the way most typical peoples do. As one of my classmates put it, it's like when you lose the Wi-Fi connection and your YouTube video stops loading. This is a really big pain in my butt. It is the reason why I can't talk or write. It is the reason why learning new skills is like running up an escalator the wrong way. This is also the reason why people think I'm not capable but I understand everything you want me to do. I always knew what I was supposed to do, but the shackles of autism restrained my responses. People need to give us more credit. It takes serious practice, but I will get it. The biggest hurdle I face is paying attention to my brain over my body. Autism controls the body. Autism lives in the brain, which makes us act differently, but don't confuse that with intelligence. I am strangled by my motor system and experience raw impulsivity. It's difficult to make my body get on the path but my goal is to have a body that is harmonious with my brain. When you encounter someone like me, don't stop teaching because we are capable of learning. We are capable of being motor superstars at our own pace. Just know we try hard every day.

6 CONCLUSION

I'm inspired by people who stand up to injustice. It gives me courage to fight like a lion for autistics every day. The best advice I can give to anyone with autism is fight for your right to be treated like you deserve to be a part of this world. To all the moms and dads, keep showering your kids with love. To all teachers, continue to work for all students with autism to have an equal education like others. To my best therapy team, you rock and you guys will change the world for autistics. Life with autism has taught me love and compassion towards everyone. To the world, compassion changes everything. The end.

AFTERWORD
By Edlyn Vallejo Peña, Ph.D.

How can I describe the feeling of witnessing your child express his complex and moving insights for the first time after years of silence? It takes your breath away. Before Diego learned to communicate his thoughts, my husband, Damien, and I loved him as deeply as we do now. But we can't say that we truly *knew* our own son. His involuntary movements, unexpected vocalizations, lack of eye contact, and difficulty following instructions clouded our understanding of his hidden intellect and spirit. We were incredibly mistaken about his capabilities. Over time, with each word he spelled and typed, Diego peeled back the layers of his personality, humor, and giftedness. We marveled at his engagement with topics about ecosystems, civil rights, and the history of peace at the age of 6. We cried during the times when he expressed heartache over his limited speech— "It's so hard" and "I sound funny." We bristled when he spelled out profanity to get our attention. We laughed when he told jokes. We admired his ambition and advocacy to "destroy old ideas on autism." After nearly four years of communicating with a letter board and keyboard, his expressive words still stun and delight us. We *know* Diego now. The world *knows* Diego now. He is no longer dismissed and invisible to others. With communication, he has a place in this world.

Admittedly, the road to securing support to teach Diego communication on a letter board and keyboard has been bumpy and chock-full of pot holes. Diego was fortunate to be introduced to Rapid Prompting Method by Soma Mukhopadhyay in Austin, Texas at a young age. At the time, few providers in our area supported Rapid Prompting Method, an educational approach that leads to communication. Some completely rejected the method all together. In fact, several providers requested that we stop our attempts at Rapid Prompting Method. We politely told them to stick their opinions where the sun doesn't shine. We didn't doubt our decision for one second. Never in a million years would we take away Diego's communication—his voice.

I often think about Diego's future. Before, I believed that what I wanted most for him was happiness. But, no, happiness is fleeting. Now, what I want more than anything is for Diego to have a purpose-filled life. One in which he actively participates in this world in a way that brings him meaning and fulfillment. That is why we have prioritized his access to communication. Without communication, opportunity and purpose are lost. Now that he meaningfully communicates, he has transitioned from a passive recipient of knowledge in a segregated special education classroom into a student leader who imparts knowledge to his typical peers in an inclusive classroom. He is an award-winning grant recipient in the Gifted and Talented Education (GATE) program. He is now the author of his first book. My wish for Diego is the same for all autistic students with limited means to communicate. Diego will make an indelible mark on this world. He will contribute in ways we can't even imagine. All autistics deserve the opportunity to become leaders and agents of change.

ALTERNATIVE COMMUNICATION RESOURCES
(Presented in alphabetical order)

BOOKS

Autism: Sensory-Movement Differences and Diversity
Martha R. Leary & Anne M. Donnellan (2014)

Carly's Voice: Breaking Through Autism
Arthur Fleischmann & Carly Fleischmann
(2012)

How Can I Talk if My Lips Don't Move?: Inside My Autistic Mind
Tito Mukhopadhyay (2008)

Ido in Autismland: Climbing Out of Autism's Silent Prison
Ido Kedar (2012)

Plankton Dreams: What I Learned in Special Ed
Tito Mukhopadhyay (2015)

The Reason I Jump: The Inner Voice of a Thirteen Year-Old Boy with Autism
Naoki Higashida (2013)

Typed Words, Loud Voices
Amy Sequencia & Elizabeth J. Grace (2015)

DOCUMENTARIES

A Mother's Courage: Talking Back to Autism
(2010)

Dillan's Voice (2016)

My Voice: One man's Journey Through the Silent World of Autism (2017)

Spectrum: A Story of the Mind (2017)

The Power of Finding Your Voice (Tedx Talk by Parisa Khosravi) (2017)

Wretches and Jabberers (2010)

ORGANIZATIONS

A.C.E. Teaching and Consulting

Autism and Communication Center, California Lutheran University

Golden Hat Foundation

Growing Kids Therapy

Helping Autism through Learning and Outreach (HALO)

Hope, Expression and Education for Individuals with Severe Disabilities (HEED)

Hussman Institute for Autism

Institute on Communication and Inclusion, Syracuse University

Optimal Rhythms/Access Academy

Reach Every Voice

Resource for Education, Advocacy,
Communication, and Housing (REACH)

RPM+ for Autism and Other Disabilities

TASH

Unlocking Voices – Using RPM

GLOSSARY

Apraxia: According to the American Speech Language Association, "Childhood apraxia of speech (CAS) is a motor speech disorder. Children with CAS have problems saying sounds, syllables, and words. This is not because of muscle weakness or paralysis. The brain has problems planning to move the body parts (e.g., lips, jaw, tongue) needed for speech. The child knows what he or she wants to say, but his/her brain has difficulty coordinating the muscle movements necessary to say those words." (http://www.asha.org/public/speech/disorders/ChildhoodApraxia/)

Augmentative and alternative communication (AAC): The American Speech Language Association defines AAC as including "all forms of communication (other than oral speech) that are used to express thoughts, needs, wants, and ideas. We all use AAC when we make facial expressions or gestures, use symbols or pictures, or write." (http://www.asha.org/public/speech/disorders/AAC/)

Motor System: The body's system that processes movement, both voluntary and involuntary.

Neurotypical: People who are not diagnosed with autism. Autistic people or people with neurological differences are sometimes referred to as neurodiverse while those without autism are neurotypical.

Talker: What people often refer to as their communication device or speech generating device.

Sensory System: The body's system that processes sensory information, like hearing, touching, seeing, tasting, and smelling.

Stimming: Short for self-stimulatory behaviors, usually meaning repetitive body movements or repetitive movement of objects.

ABOUT THE AUTHOR

At 9 years old, Diego M. Peña is a self-advocate in the making. On his agenda are disability rights, inclusion, and educating others about autism. Diego's limited ability to speak does not stop him from spreading autism acceptance and awareness through his writings and presentations. Diego uses an iPad, letter board, and key board to communicate. *Anatomy of Autism* is his first published book. He enjoys swimming, riding horses, playing on the iPad, writing short stories, and spending time with his witty dad, amazing mom, and loving grandma, Tata.

Made in the USA
San Bernardino, CA
19 April 2017